AMANDA NAIRN

AMANDA'S TALE

A Very Personal Journey through Suicide and Beyond

To order additional copies of this book, contact:
Xlibris
AU TFN: 1 800 844 927 (Toll Free inside Australia)
AU Local: 0283 108 187 (+61 2 8310 8187 from outside Australia)
www.xlibris.com.au
Orders@Xlibris.com.au

ISBN: 978-1-6641-0014-5 (sc)
ISBN: 978-1-6641-0013-8 (e)

Print information available on the last page

Rev. date: 08/25/2020

AMANDA'S TALE

A very personal journey through
suicide and beyond

Firstly, let me briefly introduce myself. I am a 56-year-old mother of three young adults in a beautiful same sex relationship with Sue, who has two children of similar age. When the kids were younger, we have lived as a big blended family, but this stopped working so well and we divided the households a few years ago.

Sue and I are competitive ballroom dancers both in Same Sex and open amateur competition. She works as a casual administrator at the dance studio. I have been unemployed for some time.

This account follows from a long-planned attempt to end my life by way of slow acting poison and a (fast acting) razor, (I will describe that more fully later) and the two-month long sojourn in the acute mental health ward at the Royal Adelaide Hospital that followed.

The account traces my progress by way of illustrated poetry that I produced along the way. While I am neither poet nor artist, this activity helped me to articulate my thoughts and feelings and, by having them stuck on my wall, gave me opportunity to evaluate them. You will see how the tone of the poetry changes, reflecting my slow recovery.

I hope you enjoy this account and find in it something that you can relate to your own experience or that of your loved ones.

The Suicide

Another day, another day goes by
I watch the arc of sun, the play of shade
I see the world through windows smeared, I lie
here in this cell, this cell that I have made

I listen to my heart, its steady beat
to spite me, beating on, I will it stop.
If hunger comes, unwanted, then I eat
My body wants to live, my mind does not
So in that mind I plan how I must flee
Divorce my future, of my life take leave.

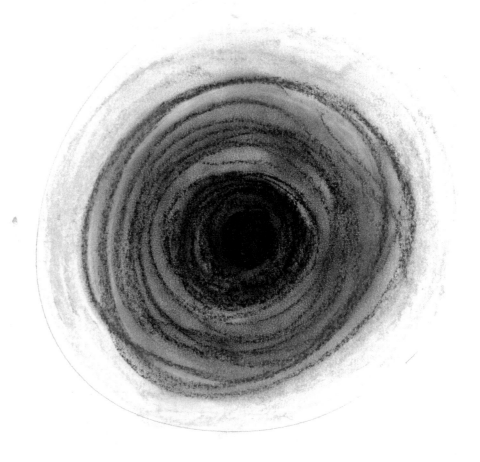

1. Plumbing the depths

> **The Suicide:**
>
> *Another day, another day goes by*
> *I watch the arc of sun, the play of shade*
> *I see the world through windows smeared, I lie*
> *Here in this cell, this cell that I have made*
> *I listen to my heart, its steady beat,*
> *To spite me beating on, I will it stop*
> *If hunger comes, unwanted, then I eat*
> *My body wants to live, my mind does not*
> *So, in that mind I plan how I must flee*
> *Divorce my future, of my life take leave*

In a deep dark hole with no way out of it, my relationship with suicide began in 2011. I found myself facing a perfect storm of overnight work, issues with the kids and the dog and a need to move to a new house (all seven of us + dog). Needing to find a house between the Sydney Dem and Mosman Primary with four bedrooms, three of them large enough for sharing, is no joke.

In any case, the stress in all of this sent me into the office of a local psychologist. I found her input so expensive both financially and emotionally that I gave up and gave myself permission to suicide.

I laid a careful plan, firstly taking out life insurance and a including a year-long stay to wait for the exclusion for self-harm to elapse. Over that year, I cultivated a habit of cliff walks on sunny days. The plan was to wait for a sunny day following the conclusion of a work contract. (i.e. with money coming in). Then to head down to the National Park walk away from any onlookers then accidentally on purpose step off, leaving open the idea that it was an accident. But when the day came, someone noticed me weeping and looking over and helpfully dialled lifeline on my behalf. Police tracked my car down, while heading home and that became my first contact with Mental Health infrastructure.

Some time later, I became aware of Wilkinson Sword razors, available in packs of 10 in every supermarket. They made it easy to open superficial veins, and I liked the sense of control and release this gave me. In fact, almost as soon as I realised this, I planned a road trip: four nights away, four veins opened. Not wanting to see how much I bled and not wanting to make a mess, I did my cutting in the shower in the evening. I let the blood flow until I started to feel ill, or just until I wanted to go to bed. Then I would staunch the flow, carefully dry off, and apply a band-aid. Sometimes that was enough, and in others I would find blood on the sheets in the morning.

After my trip I went back to Sydney to pick up Sue for a weekend in Mudgee.

"You look kind of pale" she said when I picked her up.

"I'm fine," I replied, "just haven't seen much sun lately". And I did feel basically ok. But later, walking to take photos of a nice piece of landscape, I found myself breathless and panting.

On the Sunday we went to a sort of bush dance/barbecue. We're dancers so I said, "let's dance" and we did, but after a few bars I had to sit down.

"This really isn't right," said Sue, "Soon as we're home, you're off to the doctor." I agreed, no sense in arguing.

This next day I presented to my GP who agreed to do a blood count. Back at home I went early to bed, only to have my phone ring most insistently at 2am. It was my GP.

"Your blood count is very low", she said. "you must go to the hospital right away, call an ambulance".

Of course, I argued, "I'm fine, I'll go in in the morning". But she was adamant. She said the result was 30 (normal range 90-120) and that she would tell the hospital I was coming.

The ambulance folk didn't seem very impressed – walked me out to the ambulance

Neither did the emergency team. The standing assumption seemed to be that any result that low had to be a mistake. So, they did their own test: 28. Suddenly the emergency room shifted into high gear. It would have been comical if they hadn't been so serious. I was made to lie down, heart monitors attached, a canula inserted and later, transfusions of blood and some sort of iron syrup.

After this I mostly made single cuts and was careful not to bleed too much. But the admission had roused the interest of the mental health authorities.

I acquired a psychiatrist and contact person in the outpatient mental health team, a prescription for mood control and sleep, and the services of a psychoanalyst. None of it made much difference to how I felt.

Then things went wrong. My old friend and the head of the consulting business I had been sourcing work through, let me know that my services would no longer be required

Recognising how this development ramped up my personal risk, I did my best to bounce back, diving into a master's program in learning and leadership with a view to going into corporate training roles. I enjoyed this and did well finishing with a level of enthusiasm for me to continue and do a PhD. Unfortunately, though, I found that the sorts of role I was interested in were not interested in my master's and many specified the requirement for a vocational qualification in Training and Assessment. And I couldn't afford to stay on and do the PhD.

I completed the vocational qualification in January of the following year but was still getting nowhere with raising employer interest. I started to lose hope, and as I did so, the idea of divorcing my future developed in my mind. I started to disregard problems and issues occurring beyond the immediate future and stopped looking forward to anything at all. None of it seemed relevant to me.

Against that background I experimented with rat poison. I swallowed one pack because I had noticed it in Bunnings. Then, recognising how much bigger I am than the average rat, swallowed a second pack. It wasn't hard, and for a week or so, nothing happened. I didn't know what to expect from the poison so concluded that I had not taken enough. A slow nosebleed started. Several days later it was Mardi Gras and I was due to go out to dinner. But my nose was still dripping so I went to the hospital to get the cauterisation done, my GP having refused to do it herself.

At the hospital, I was taken into emergency and a blood test was taken. An ENT[1] doctor took me into a treatment room and was peering into my nose, when a tap came at the door. The ENT excused herself and went out. When she came back, she said "That was about you", "do you know why your clotting factors are so low? Your INR[2] is 14 when it should be 1!"

---

1 Ear, Nose and Throat

2 **INR** stands for International Normalised Ratio, also referred to as Prothrombin time (PT), and is a standardised measurement of the time it takes for blood to clot. A normal score is 1.0 and very high scores may lead to the spontaneous bleeding that I was experiencing.

I did not: In taking the rat poison, I had not been interested in exploring the likely symptomology of it. So, when nothing much had happened save the nosebleed in five or six days, I assumed I had not taken enough. I did not connect the irritating nosebleed to the poison, so there was a bit of confusion before I put 2 and 2 together and confessed to the rat poison. They made me stay. So much for Mardi Gras, so much for the dinner! I was treated in emergency and then moved to the Acute Assessment Ward – the modern version of a padded cell.

I left there a week or so later, retaining a level of enthusiasm for rat poison. I now knew that rat poison is a long lasting and accumulative blood thinner like warfarin, causing internal and external bleeding in high enough concentration. I imagine that would be nasty for the rats, but for me, the idea of uncontrolled bleeding held some appeal.

Oh Hollow Me.

Oh Hollow me
a shell all told
of agence, nought
not calm, not told

Oh Hollow me
of draining funds
long unemployed
with no demand

Oh Hollow me
costs unbound
for rent for food
coin must be found

Oh Hollow me
I cannot stay
can't navigate
to brighter day.

2. Planning the Escape

Oh, Hollow Me

Oh, hollow me
A shell all told
Of agency, nought
not calm, not bold

Oh, Hollow me
Of draining funds
long unemployed
with no demand

Oh, hollow me
Of costs unbound
for rent, for food
coin must be found

Oh, Hollow Me
I cannot stay
Can't navigate
To brighter day

The poem and image reflect my sense of inadequacy and hopelessness. Feeling hollow and beset by costs and interventions beyond my control and unable to do anything to improve my situation.

The image shows the figure in negative space, picked out by the myriad of forces acting on it, otherwise there would be no figure at all.

My experience with rat poison told me that Sue would certainly notice any symptoms of such poisoning, so I understood that I would have to be away from home and away from Sue to take the rat bate and see the symptoms develop. I knew that 5 or 6 days after taking it some bleeding would be likely, and S would immediately and correctly suggest that I had poisoned myself with rat bate again.

So, when my mother suggested that, for my birthday, we might meet up in Adelaide for a scenic flight over Lake Ayres – then in flood, I saw an opportunity: I would drive down to the Head of the Bight, there to see the annual visit of whales to mate and give birth, and then drive on to meet Mum in Adelaide. On the way down, I would swallow five packs of rat bait, one per day, knowing that it would take 4 or 5 days for symptoms to begin.

After the flight, I planned to drive back to Mt Grenfell Historic Park. This is a beautiful spot and, once there I would walk away from the marked trail and inflate an air mattress brought for the purpose. The next step would be to open a few superficial veins and lie down to let exsanguination[3] take its course.

I was excited to be going, both for the whales, my mother and the flight, as well as for my plan to not return.

This was the plan.

---

3 Exsanguination – fatal blood loss

Gorgon

I walking dead
Envivenned by my hearts persistent beat
A Rhythm to lend purpose to my cause
A beat to bring a meaning to my breath
But why should it & why should I
Draw breath still in this still room

I've lived enough, my time is done
I beg my heart be still.

3. The Attempt

> **Be Still**
>
> *I walking dead*
> *Enlivened by my heart's persistent beat*
> *A rhythm to lend purpose to my cause*
> *a beat to bring meaning to my breath*
> *But why should it and why should I*
> *Draw breath still in this still room*
> *I've lived enough, my time is done*
> *I beg my heart be still*

The word in pink was an accidental transfer but it reads "Corazon'" the Spanish word for Heart, also used as a term of endearment, so quite appropriate for this poem.

As the day for my departure grew closer, I became more and more wrapped up in my plan. It was as if I was in a sort of parallel universe with only me in it. Others, my therapist, my partner and children, seemed hardly to exist, so wrapped was I in my own escape capsule.

So, I drove down to the whales, which were lovely. And swallowed the poison one pack per day, washed down with water, which was surprisingly easy.

I was there for two days and on each day, there were whales pretty much wherever you looked and the odd pod of dolphins frolicking in the shallower water. The weather, despite it being winter, was brilliant and a crisp sea breeze ruffled the water and the mostly blue and grey hair dos of my fellow tourists.

The whales which had given birth looked like nothing so much as a semi submerged full size buses with a minibuses cavorting around them. Other whales were solitary and looking for a mate, like this one posing for photographs.

After two days with the whales, I was still symptom free and hoped they would hold off for long enough. I was glad I had taken the poison and was looking forward to the conclusion of my plan.

I headed off to Adelaide to meet my mother.

I was still symptom free when I got to Adelaide, and my mother and I joined a light plane sized group for the scenic flight. This included an overflight over the mysterious Maree Man as well as the lakes and came with lunch in the Birdsville pub. We talked about all sorts of things as we went. Among them, I raised a question that had been bothering me.

"you know how there was a family story about me being a black and blue baby and possibly brain damaged. What actually happened?"

Mum looked a bit surprised but collected her thoughts and replied, "Yes, you were a face presentation and they let the labour go on far too long before deciding they should do a Caesar. But as it happened, when they moved me to a theatre bed, you tucked your chin in and were born naturally. But you were terribly bruised, we both were."

From me: "now I understand what happened. So, what was it like when we went home"?

"It was very difficult. You were in pain and miserable and couldn't suck properly for the first few weeks and your father didn't know what to do with himself. Neither did I. It took me a few weeks to recover from your birth as well."

I stood up and went over and hugged her. "Thank you, I kind of needed to know that"

After that we talked about many other things and had a lovely day together.

As I farewelled her and drove away, symptoms kicked off with a slow nosebleed and a series of oral blood blisters. Driving on, spontaneous bruising started to appear on my face, legs and trunk, and a constellation of small bleeding petechiae (spots) opened up on my front and back. Later at a motel on the way I noted that my faeces had turned to a tar like substance and my urine, rose gold. It became very difficult not to bleed on the bedsheets, and I used a bath sheet towel to try to shield them.

As I drove north, bleeding a little bit from a lot of places, but still feeling pretty much okay, I found that my sense of encapsulation in my plans started to erode. Up until that time I had been single mindedly committed to the plans that I had made and had welcomed each emerging symptom. But now I started to debate myself:

"What sort of harm would my disappearance and demise cause to my children, Sue and my mother?"

"Or would my death end their long experience of my self-harm and attempted suicide. And would this afford them a measure of relief?"

Of course, I wanted to believe the second contention, while of course, the harm would have been severe.

With this internal dialogue ongoing, I drove into Wilcannia – my last stop before Mt Grenfell. The proprietor of the motel looked concerned at my appearance but didn't say anything. The facial bruising and nosebleed made me look as if I had been beaten up. However, the following morning, as I dropped off the room key, She and a cleaner took up gentle position in front of my car.

"Love, you look like you need to get some help", "the motel owner said

"And whoever it was that hurt you will get what's coming to him", added the cleaner

The motel owner looked her companion over. "All in good time", she said, "she needs to go to the hospital first".

Gently, they shepherded me towards the base hospital.

By this stage, I concluded that the universe had conspired in favour of my children and loved ones, and I confessed to the rat poison. At the base hospital they tried to measure my INR, but it turned out to be above the range the little measuring machine could handle. I think I broke it. In the end, they concluded that I needed more than they could offer at the base hospital, they called Adelaide, gave me a parting shot of vitamin K and sent me back down to Adelaide with the Flying Doctor, thence by ambulance to the Royal Adelaide. The single shot of K stopped my nose bleed, which seemed almost magical.

There, I was treated in emergency for 2 or 3 days until the bleeding stopped and clotting returned to normal, and then moved into 'G2', the acute mental health care ward.

4. Life on the Ward

The Cell

Here lying in the cell that I have made
I found an exit door that I could take
But with it came the guilt so thickly laid
I balked and sealed the padlock on my cage
So, stand for me those dreadful walls
Of marching costs and dwindling funds
Unwanted skills, and Idle hands
A narrow space err closer draws
I need a way to leave my cage of woe
To break its walls or simply just to go

This poem reflects my state of mind as I arrived at the G2 Mental Ward in Adelaide I had failed to go through with my plan, and now found myself in a cell of my own making – in the G2 ward. I was filthy with myself, furious that I had accepted the help of the kind Wilcannia ladies. Furious that I had not gone through with the plan. And that had left me 'caged', facing all the same issues that I started with.

I arrived on the ward by wheelchair, even though I was well able to walk myself, and taken into a sort of a reception room. There I was left a few minutes, a lock turned on the door until a nurse, Linda, walked in. "Well", she said, "you ---------must be Amanda, we've heard a lot about you".

"Oh", I said, "I guess you know what I did to get here".

"Yes, but don't worry about that, we're just here to help you". "The first thing we have to do is take your photo so that security know who you are"

She produced a large digital camera and indicated I stand in front of a bare section of wall. She took a shot and frowned

"Perhaps turn your head a little to the right so we can't see the bruising so much"

I did so and the resultant image was judged adequate and the camera set aside.

"Ok," she said, "first things first, we don't have any belts, straps or shoelaces on the ward". I was quickly divested of my shoelaces and the tie for my trousers and then, holding my pants up and shuffling to keep my shoes on with my toes, she led me out into the corridor.

"I'll show you around', she said, "but don't you have any other clothes?".

I didn't know what had happened to the bag I had been travelling with, or my computer bag and suspected that both were still in my car in Wilcannia. "No", I said "I don't think so".

"I'll see what we can do. We can usually find something".

In the meantime, we circled the facility: a large dining room, two courtyards, three televisions, a pool table, a table tennis table, a gym, an art room, a 'library' room with a supply of books, games and jigsaw puzzles, and a couple of "Comfort Rooms" containing massage chairs. I was fully occupied with keeping my pants and shoes on, so didn't make any contact with the other patients I saw on the way. That would come later.

The room I was led to had its own facilities and a desk area and was fetchingly decorated with landscapes overpainted on large scale maps. To foil any attempt at hanging, the bathroom doors were salon style and hung by magnets in place of regular hinges.

Later that day Linda reappeared in my room with a selection of basic items: shirts, undies, pants and toiletries including a pack of hair ties. I am short haired so wondered about these until realising that they were just what was needed to keep lace-less shoes on feet.

Linda and the other nurses were friendly, each allocated to 4 or 5 patients each day, but I saw most of Linda and I grew to like her a lot

I quickly found out that there was a weekly calendar of activities: art, music, walking and cooking. I went to most of them, but in particular liked the art groups. I had been writing poetry in a bid to articulate and explain how I was feeling. In art groups I attached images to emphasise the articulations. The resultant posters I stuck to my walls for further consideration, and now form the structure for this account. You have already seen a few of them. More on these later.

Patients leave provisions ranged from none at all to half days and even full days. I was initially under tight leave provisions – none or half an hour if accompanied by a responsible adult. As I was in Adelaide and away from friends and family, these were thin on the ground where I was concerned. Later I had 3X30 minutes unaccompanied, and even a special leave to accompany a colleague to see his work in an exhibition in the city.

For me, I found periods of restriction to the ward especially difficult, practically missing such commonplace things as coffee and the chance to move around without being tracked. But also intensely feeling my separation from my friends and family and a squirrely sense of incarceration. I had managed to keep a few of the blades I had with me in Wilcannia, and I am sorry to say that at such times I was sorely tempted to use them, and a few times I did so.

But with only a half hour of leave, I could get a coffee and visit the duck pond next to the hospital, becoming quite well acquainted with ducks and peahens that lived there.

At the ward, the resident doctors considered my existing drug regime and made some changes to improve the likely mood stabilisation delivered. They also prescribed ECT (electroconvulsive therapy). Who knew that was still a thing!? Immediate views from One Flew Over the Cuckoo's' Nest sprung to mind. My alarm must have shown as they immediately explained that 'modern' ECT took place under general anaesthetic and with a muscle relaxant.

Thus reassured, I was happy to do try Electro Convulsive Therapy and was guardedly hopeful.

I go towards my end tonight
a brighter day to find
and now I hold myself in fright
a bolt to clear my mind
Too long I've wandered in the dark
too oft my blood set free
too many razors, poisons stark
too dark to dark to see
So now I hope the current's flow
will bring the sun rise

where I go

5. My Experience of ECT

> ***ECT***
>
> *I go towards my end tonight*
> *A brighter day to find*
> *And now I hold myself in fright*
> *a bolt to clear my mind*
> *Too long I 've wandered in the dark*
> *too many razors, poisons stark*
> *Too dark, too dark to see*
> *So now I hope the current's flow*
> *Will bring the sunrise where I go*

The image shows a sunrise, echoing the poems imagery. It also shows the prevailing darkness of both sea and sky into which the sunrise is introduced. It shows my guarded hope that the treatment would relieve the overwhelming darkness of my world view.

Incidentally, the first line "I go toward my end tonight" on this occasion refers not to my death but the hope that that night would mark the end of the suicidal, self-harming phase of my life.

The ECT program was administered on an outpatient basis at the Ramsey Clinic, a dedicated psychiatric facility linked to the university of Adelaide. This meant that there were frequently young trainee doctors in the corners, observing the process. According to the Clinics own statement of services:

"**Electro Convulsive Therapy** is used in the treatment of severe depressive illness, mania and other forms of psychosis. The ECT suite has state of the art facilities and is staffed by Registered Nurses experienced in post anaesthetic recovery".

My repeated suicide attempts and self-harm qualified me for the program through the diagnosis of severe depressive illness.

The therapy was applied three days a week, Monday, Wednesday and Friday, starting with what was known as 'Ultra Brief' treatment.

An ECT day started with an early, pre-breakfast ride to the clinic, followed by a brief wait in their sunbathed waiting area. At the beginning I had another patient receiving the therapy with me, and we took turns at going first. They would put in a cannula in the waiting area, then bring in a bed and wheel me into the treatment room. If there were students present, they were then introduced and asked if I minded them being there (I didn't). Then they administered a short acting general anaesthetic and a muscle relaxant.

After the treatment I would wake up in a recovery room, mentally quite blank about what had happened and why. In this state, we were given breakfast – I developed a liking for Weetabix. The blankness filled in quite quickly and I was usually up to speed by the time we were headed back to the ward in the Royal Adelaide and did not notice any long-standing memory issues.

For the first few times I was also quite still and sore and enjoyed the massage chairs in the so-called comfort rooms.

Dark Light

My skull, my skull, that fragile shell
Thrice cracked each week
To draw the light
And draw me from my darker past
And let a dark light shine

I meant this to be a positive image of the 'dark light' shining, though my therapist does point out that there is a lot of black paint there too (some of which I have trimmed away.)

I enjoyed the process of having ECT and in this period generated a number of broadly positive images, with or without lines of verse. An example is the one shown of the profound light cast by an Asian stye fishing lantern

After 9 sessions of ultrabrief therepy, my doctors were not satisfied with my progess. I was moved to right unilateral placement, deemed likely to produce stronger, more effective convulsions. However, with this change I started to observe stronger impacts on my effective memory.

This display shows my dawning understanding that the ECT was having a significant impact on my memory, while the short poem reflects the intended purpose of the ECT process. The blue checked walkway represents the legal formality of being 'scheduled'

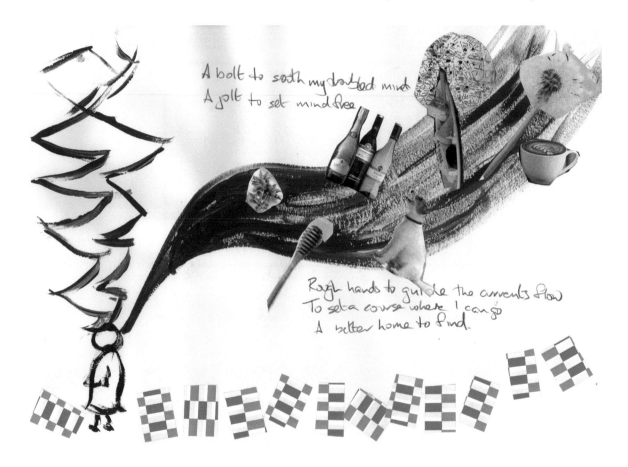

> *A bolt to soothe my troubled mind*
> *A jolt to set mind free*
> *Rough hands to guide the current's flow*
> *To set a course where I could go*
> *A better home to find*

Submit that I might find a light
A light to light my way
To bring my future into light
And turn my light to day
But can I credit such a claim
So close & dark I find.
The future dark & drear, the same
As ever, clouded mind
And things that wait there cause me fear
Why would I want them brought oft clear

6. Dawning Darkside

> *Submit that I might find a light*
> *A light to light my way*
> *To bring my future into light*
> *And turn my night to day*
> *But can I credit such a claim*
> *So close and dark I find*
> *The future dark and drear the same*
> *As ever clouded mind*
> *And things that lurk there cause me fear*
> *Why would I want them brought out clear?*

Weeks passed and I came to suspect that the ECT was not having the expected impact on my depressive symptoms. My guarded enthusiasm gave way to concern about both my memory and what the ECT could be expected to deliver. In particular I did not want it to shine any kind of light into the murky depths of my subconcious. . In pshycoanalysis I had come to understand something of the role of early trauma in my reactions and general depressive state. This entailed some carefully guarded and very painful memories. I had no desire to revisit these with the Adelaide doctors and was increasingly worried that I might have to.

My memory problems also became obvious. I couldn't bring to mind my address, email address, phone number, how the phone worked. I couldn't recall the floor plan of my house, or how many times my long-term psychoanalist had visited me in the Adelaide ward. I couldn't remember what else I couldn't remember. That frightnned me.

The Doctors agreed to finish the ECT after 15 sessions over six weeks. I was not part of tha decision and it left me feeling defeated. My memory had been impacted and I had had little or no contact with psychiatrists or psychologists over the period that I had been having the treatment.

Over that time I had succumbed to temptation a couple of times and engaged in self-harm by way of a razor blade applied to a superficial vein on hands or feet. This had earned me placement on level one ITO (Interim Treatment Order) which meant 24 hour one-on-one observation for short periods – requiring a nurse to follow around and sit in the room overnight. This was followed by restriction to the ward for much of my stay. As mentioned previously, this was very frustrating..[4]

---

4 Superficial meaning just under the skin and not paired with an artery

Memento of the ECT

With 15 times the ECT
I found the jolts had shattered me
A million shards, my memory
Both what I thought and how to be
Was glad to set the dark thoughts free
But scared to find me all at sea
With apps and emails lost to me
Numbers, names dissorderly
Memento of the ECT

WHY

What use am I, a waste of space
Am held here, nowhere, hopelessly
Am tethered here, what point in mind?
What meaning am I meant to find
& they that love me can not know
How far I've gone, how far to go
To far to ever make it home
So far from who I've been I've gone
Just how am I supposed to heal
when drawn to death is all I
feel

A. Nairn

7. A way ahead

> ### *Why*
>
> *What use am I a waste of space?*
> *Am held here, nowhere hope is kept*
> *Am tethered here, what point in mind*
> *What meaning am I meant to find*
> *and They that love me cannot know*
> *How far I've come, how far to go*
> *Too far to ever make it home*
> *So far from who I've been, I've gone*
> *Just how am I supposed to heal*
> *When drawn to death is all I feel*

I made this exhibit for what was, for me, a completely novel purpose. I wrote it for my doctors to give as clear a picture as I could about how I was feeling. So, I brought it with to my next meeting with the doctor and gave it to Dr Rossario to read. He took his time reading it and then looked across to me

"Well it's good that you could write it, and good that you could show it to me", he paused, "better out than in". Then it was put aside.

But laying down my thoughts for someone else to read made me really look at my wall of illustrated poetry in a new way. The repeated jolts from the ETC had not just shaken loose my memory, they had also shaken loose my ownership of the ideas I had presented and illustrated. I could still read and understand my efforts, but I found that I no longer occupied or owned them. I could consider them without falling into them. I could agree with myself to put them aside.

The ECT had, in effect, shaken out the ideas underlying self-harming behaviour. Not flushing them away, but rather, like a simple dropped jigsaw, still there in their constituent parts, visible, able to be articulated. It was subject to an act of will to either pick them up, reassemble and reclaim them, or to have done with them once and for all.

This was my first and largest step on my way to recovery.

As I worked through this task, I became increasingly aware of the support and sheer kindness of the nursing staff and others working in the G2 ward. On one occasion, I walked in on the cleaners working in my room. They welcomed me and said, "we love doing your room, we can't wait to see if you have got any further with your jigsaw or if there are any new pictures on your wall".

"I don't always understand them, but you write lovely poems".

My first response was horror that they had been reading them, but this was chased out by a small warm glow of pride. Another first for me!

Knowing that plans for my release where in the works, I decided to do a thankyou poster that had a bit of space for personal messages. It was aimed at the nurses, doctors, group convenors and cleaners. Everyone who had been so kind. A nurse kindly copied it through for me.

I came here lost and battle scarred

A casualty of inner wars

I found here refuge, safe and rare

To treat my wounds and sooth my scars

And found here kindness, myriad forms

Both medical and personal

So

Thank you all, you showed the way

For me to find my brighter day

Of course, the ECT and the kindly staff where not the only thing that helped with my eventual recovery.

As I mentioned, the duck pond next to the hospital was a place of calm and peace for me. There were a pair of peahens raising their four peachicks and a pair of ducks. After I had observed them for a while, I think the ducks were both young males, perhaps chicks of the previous season and yet to establish their own families. At times, other ducks dropped in, which helped solidify that view. The pea chicks though, were a joy to watch, often calling to each other, or playing follow the leader round the pond. I enjoyed them so much I made a picture of them.

More generally, I believe that access to the natural environment of the wetland park was a huge benefit to me, and one that I think would be an asset for any mental facility. The G2 had two courtyards with minimal garden. I would have been wonderful to plant one out to provide bird habitat, or flowers, or food plants. The care of such plantings could be an option available to residents.

A second thing that helped, indirectly, was the pool table. It facilitated, in the later part of my stay, making friends with the irrepressible Karen and through her, Jeremy. Jeremy is a beautiful soul and an artist, and it was through talking to him that I began to step outside the dark and stormy world of my own conscious mind. I don't think he knows the role he played in bringing me back to life, but I thank him from the bottom of my soul.

Thirdly, jigsaw puzzles. If you like that sort of thing, nothing fills in time quite like it. I did a couple of big ones, as mentioned, admired by the cleaners.

An obvious fourth was the bi-weekly art group. You will know by now that I am no sort of artist, but the group provided the tools I needed to illustrate and add depth to the verses that had been bubbling out of me from the start. George who ran the groups and provided the materials, was supportive of my efforts without ever asking to read the verse. This allowed me to continue to try to articulate my reality without any filtering.

Finally, I began to recognise that I had a few useful skills: I could teach an approach to simple poetry (like my own) that most people could manage[5]. Or, I could teach dance. Unfortunately, I was transferred back to Sydney before these could be organised.

---

5 Simple approach to lay poetry described at the back of this document

8. Home Bound

> ### *Homeward Bound*
>
> *I brought my blood*
> *I brought my scars*
> *I brought my sore and troubled mind*
> *But then, I brought some interest too*
> *With runs of words*
> *And painted daubs*
> *And watched the daily life of birds*
> *And through these, and the doctors' words*
> *I found a door where I could go*

My mother and my brother came from Perth to take charge of me on my release and conduct me back up to Sydney.

But this was not without its own drama. Aware that I was embarking on a whole new phase of my life, I used a blade that I had secreted away to cut for the last time. In the shower on the last night but one, I found a prominent vein on my wrist, about the level of my watch strap, and sliced cleanly across it. It bled impressively and I let it. It left me feeling rather faint, but I stopped it eventually stopped the bleeding, applied a band aid and went to bed.

The next morning (my last day) blood was taken for discharge tests. I was going about my business when one of the nurses I didn't know so well came puffing up. "Come with me", she said, "your blood count is so low that you need to have a transfusion!". I followed meekly and was walked over to emergency and to an emergency bed.

Once there a doctor came in. "So, have you been bleeding from anywhere? Nosebleeds, tarry facies, blood in your urine?". I told him about the cut and showed it to him. He frowned, "I don't think you could have bled that much through that little cut". Then he ordered an endoscopy and a cat scan.

Meanwhile, the pathologists were struggling to figure out what kind of blood to give me, given that I have somewhat unusual blood antibodies. In the event, the transfusion didn't start till about 9 pm that evening, and proceeded to about 3 in the morning with each hour punctuated with sets of observations.

By the morning I was exhausted, but my blood count was close to normal and the emergency doctors discharged me.

Amazingly (to me), the G2 doctors agreed that the cut was unlikely to be the cause of the low count and went ahead with the discharge. I was released into the custody of my mother and brother following a conference to define the terms of release (to include my voluntary admission to the psych ward at the Royal North Shore).

I was glad to be seeing the last of the Royal Adelaide and was looking forward to a properly hot shower, or bath, a dark bedroom not regularly checked on, a glass of wine perhaps, and food with chillies. But it was not to be. When we arrived in Sydney at about six in the evening my mother thought it best to report immediately to the Royal North Shore. We got there about 7 pm.

There had been communications between the Royal Adelaide and Royal North Shore to explain that I would be turning myself in for voluntary admission and to request that they please admit me. But despite this, I was made to run the gauntlet of the emergency department triage. This took hours and it was nearing midnight before I found myself facing the Mental Health duty doctor. I was beyond tired and could barely follow his questions or keep awake to answer them. Eventually he relented and admitted me to their mental health ward. I had been there before, so passed on the offer of an orientation tour, eventually falling into bed at about 2 am.

The Sydney ward has much the same resources as the Adelaide one, less the cycle of activities (art, music, cooking etc). But I did not have much time to miss them. After just a couple of days, the Sydney doctors judged that I was well enough to be released. I was a little bit surprised at this, but grateful at the opportunity to regain control over my life. Also, a little apprehensive of what I would find waiting for me at home, where my oldest son (not overly houseproud) had had the care of my two young cats and elderly dog.

Well, in the event, the house needed a good clean out, but the animals were fine and happy to see me, as was my oldest son. My brother and his wife headed out to Wilcannia to collect my car and my mother camped out in a nearby motel and helped with the cleanout.

And so, the next stage of my recovery got underway. I see a psychoanalyst three times and week and am in weekly contact with the North Short Community Mental Health team. My Beautiful girlfriend keeps a close eye on me. My children help whenever they are asked, and I derive great joy from the three animals.

I leave you now. Still with work to do, but with the outline of a possible future for me gradually coming into view.

I thank you and wish you well.

1. Have a think about the thing you want to write about
2. Take a large piece of blank paper and write down everything you can think of associated with the thing you are writing about - words, phases, ideas – anything – fill the page
3. Put it in a drawer overnight
4. Then look at it and take a fresh sheet of paper
5. What words and phrases have resonance for you?
6. Try out different combinations. Put them together in a way that says what you mean to say
7. Read it out loud, are the rhythms pleasing? Substitute words/phrases to improve the rhythm

➤ Don't force lines to rhyme
➤ Small rhymes within a line can be very effective
➤ Don't force your work into a formal structure of words and/or lines
➤ Make sure that what you write is meaningful for you

Printed in the United States
By Bookmasters